New Forge Press
951 New Forge Road II
Ancram, New York 12502

Book designer: Sarah Smith, Small Editions
Printed in the United States of America

ISBN: 978-0-9895656-1-5

Rolling Up the Rug
An American Irish Story

The Scanlon family, 1943.
Gus, John, Michael, Mary and Mamie.

Michael Scanlon

This book is for
Mary Anne

Man is in love and loves what vanishes,
What more is there to say?
W. B. Yeats

God gave us memory so we could
have roses in winter.
J. M. Barrie

Rolling Up the Rug

The fall of 1961. I am with my father. He has returned to his homeland for the first time after 35 years in America. The two of us stand silently under a sullen Irish sky in the high, dry grass among the fallen stones of the old country farm house in County Sligo, Ireland where he was born and raised. He is quiet for a long time. As he leads me down a deserted dirt road, he shakes his head slowly, "You see that crossroads, Mick?" he points, "Oh, the life that used to be had there of a Sunday morning after Mass, the boys and girls, the laughter, the flipping of coins and the gambling, and my own father among them. Those good times — all gone."

Good times — but not good enough to keep my father from leaving the land of his birth. In 1928, a year before the depression, at age 22, he boarded the USS California at the port of County Derry and landed in New York City where he spent the rest of his life. The woman he married, my mother,

Mamie Gallagher, had arrived in New York one year before him. She was the oldest of five children and, at age 16, said goodbye to her family and her home in County Leitrim. She never saw her parents again.

My father was an Irish fiddler. My mother sang in a lilting, operatic voice. They were the life of every gathering, and they threw many a party themselves. When I think back on my parents and the apartment where they raised my brother, sister and me all those years ago, I think first about those parties.

A Saturday morning in the early 1950's. Mom and Pop begin pushing the couch, chairs and tables from the living room into the bedrooms. Getting down on their knees in the living room, they start the ritual that truly signals a night of music and dancing: *rolling up the rug*. With grunts and lots of, "Easy does it there!" they hoist the big well-worn, maroon patterned rug and banish it to the bedroom for the night. Then they rim the bare living room with bridge chairs rented for the occasion — and the room transforms into a tiny dance hall.

Later, my mother shops for a juicy ham, cold cuts, potato and macaroni salads and coleslaw from the German delicatessen. At the Jewish bakery she buys loaves of seeded rye bread, marble cake and macaroon cookies. The Highbridge Beer Distributor arrives with a keg of beer that is hauled up five flights of stairs and set on its side in the kitchen sink with a spigot attached for the pouring. Bottles of Four Roses and Canadian Club whiskey stand ready on the kitchen table to be mixed with ginger ale for "high balls."

By evening the men and women arrive decked out in their best. The Irish who lived in and around our Bronx neighborhood had come to America in the 1920's in a wave of immigration after Ireland gained independence. They were mostly from the west of Ireland, from the counties of Galway, Mayo, Sligo, Clare, Leitrim, Donegal, Roscommon, Longford, Cavan, Cork and Kerry.

The women come bustling into our little apartment all perfumed, powdered and corseted into dresses dotted with rhinestones. The men in starched white shirts with wide ties tightly knotted, their faces shiny, clean-shaven and smiling. Their big, ham-fisted-laboring-man-hands extend in greeting, crushing a dollar bill into the hand of the little boy who carries their coats and fedoras off to the bedroom.

My uncle John, the bartender at Leo

My father practicing his fiddle before a party.

3

Sullivan's Saloon, serves the drinks and before long my father, with his red and yellow bow tie, takes his seat next to Mike Ryan, the accordionist, and they strike up the first dance of the evening. It is always the same lilting melody: "The Stack of Barley" — the original Irish tune that gave birth to America's "Turkey in the Straw." At once, men and women are up on the improvised dance floor swinging each other, laughing, dancing and whooping. They stomp the bare floor of our living room while others stand around clapping their hands, tapping their feet, shouting encouragement. My father's elbow gyrates wildly on the fiddle, his left foot tapping the floor to the driving rhythm of the music. Highland flings lead into an Irish hopped-up version of the "Verse of Vienna," followed by set dances and old time waltzes. And one special night, as the fiddle and accordion music floats out our window onto the steamy summer night air, my Aunt Margaret – in a pink satin dress, her curly blond hair piled high on her head – leads the entire crowd around every room of the apartment in a Conga line that goes on forever.

Later in the evening, they settle down to sing. Happily crammed together into our Bronx apartment, these country people – now transformed into hard working New Yorkers – begin to recall the quiet beauties of the land they left behind.

Home parties where Irish immigrants created their own fun after a hard work week were popular in the 1940's and 50's. Mamie and Gus Scanlon are in the bottom row – third and fourth from the left.

They sing of the valleys, streams, and meadows of their youth:

> *Come by the hills to the land where fancy is free*
> *And stand where the peaks meet the sky*
> *And the rocks meet the sea.*

Then my mother sings:

> *Last night I had a pleasant dream*
> *I woke up with a smile*
> *I dreamt that I was home again*
> *In dear old Erin's Isle.*

For most of these people, going home again to Ireland remains only a dream.

They sing funny songs too about Eliza's Two Big Feet and of Paddy McGinty's Goat — famous for eating up all of Kate's "folderols" upon her wedding night. And then, always towards the end, my mother and father sing "their" song together. She in her chair, hands on her lap, a big, white smile on her face, him standing beside her, his hand resting on her shoulder, the roomful of friends in rapt attention, knowing well the song about to be sung:

> When you and I were seventeen,
> Life was but a dream
> The world was just a field of green
> And you my charming queen.
> Oh, do you recall
> When love was all
> And we were seventeen.

In the glow of such moments, my ten year old self wishes that nobody will go home, the lights will never go out, nothing will ever change, and nobody will ever die.

The High Bridge as it looked when it was built by Irish immigrants in 1848 making it the oldest bridge in New York. It was designed as an aqueduct carrying water from the upstate Croton Reservoir to the citizens of New York City. Photo courtesy of the United States Library of Congress's Prints and Photographs division.

The High Bridge as it looks today. In 1928, in order to improve navigation in the Harlem River, the five masonry arches that spanned the river were demolished and replaced with a single steel arch. We knew it as "the foot bridge" since no vehicles were allowed. Photo courtesy of Thaddeus Roan.

Highbridge, The Bronx

"The neighborhood where I was born was part of the city not easily come to, moated by the Harlem River along the west and unentered by the el to the east; between them it rose like some backward green garden of hills, original rocks, grass, trees, small cornfields. It was known as Highbridge after a footbridge high over the river. In its midst was a broad barren hill, which went rollicking down to a tar road under a rank of old trees, and in their shade stood a handful of narrow wooden houses yoked together, three families high, each house with its grace note of picket fence."

— From A Mass For The Dead, memoir

by William Gibson

Like William Gibson, author of *The Miracle Worker*, I am a native of Highbridge.

When I first read Gibson's lyrical description of my old neighborhood from the 1920's, I hardly recognized it as the place where I was born and raised in the 1940's and 50's. By the time my generation came along, some wooden houses were still yoked together on certain leafy streets, but I don't recall picket fences and, as for cornfields, they were something of the past. The broad barren hill Gibson describes was still there though. We called it Brown's Hill. It was a sunny place where older Italian and Irish men played bocce ball on warm summer evenings and where youngsters first learned to climb a tree or swing a baseball bat.

Like many outlying neighborhoods in New York City, Highbridge became more populated in the late 1920's and 30's as the subway and elevated train lines expanded farther uptown from the center of New York City's metropolis. The actual High Bridge spanning the Harlem River from the Bronx to Washington Heights in Manhattan originally served as an aqueduct carrying water from the upstate Croton reservoir to the people of the city. The bridge built by Irish immigrants in 1848—twelve years before the Civil War—was modeled after ancient Roman aqueducts and is the oldest bridge in New York City. I recall many a summer's afternoon standing on that foot bridge and looking down the river into the hazy distance where the tall skyscrapers rose up in Manhattan. At such a sight it was easy enough to believe what our Irish parents told us: we lived in the greatest city in the world.

Our neighborhood was set high on a bluff with streets called Summit and Woodycrest reflecting its elevated location. Other streets were named for the original English families who once owned farms in the area: Nelson, Ogden, Anderson. Plimpton Avenue was named after the family of author George Plimpton. Jerome Avenue, located at the base of our hilly neighborhood, was named after Winston Churchill's mother's family, though Jenny Jerome herself lived in Manhattan.

Highbridge was a friendly, working class neighborhood in those days, mostly of Jewish and Irish families with a sprinkling of Italian and German Americans. Men like my father went off to work in the transit, called the "railroad," while others worked in the garment district, the construction trades, or as policemen and firemen. Most families lived in five or six-story apartment houses built in the 1930's which teemed with children of all ages and sizes.

Catholic children attended Sacred Heart School. The boys at Sacred Heart were educated by the Christian Brothers, also known as the De La Salle Brothers, and the girls by the Sisters of Mercy. Boys and girls were taught separately. In my 8th grade class of 1952 over 300 boys and girls graduated. We were a thriving school in a thriving parish. "Red and white, Fight! Fight! Fight!" was our rallying cry at basketball games and track meets which we won more often than not. In mental arithmetic competitions and spelling bees held among the city's Catholic schools, we also captured a fair share of trophies.

Catholic school was free in those days. Parents paid no tuition because the prosperous parish supported the school. On Sundays, Sacred Heart Church fairly burst at the seams with hourly Masses beginning at 6 a.m. and not ending until the early afternoon. To accommodate the overflow of parishioners, an annex church, St. Eugene's with its grotto devoted to the Blessed Mother, was built at the farther end of the parish. The hard working men and women who filled these Sunday Masses felt pride in their parish and gave generously to support it with their dimes, quarters and dollars which they poured into the collection baskets every week. Sacred Heart church was a mighty fortress where everything important happened: Baptisms, Holy Communions, Confirmations, graduations, novenas, weddings and funerals.

Working class as we were, it was hard to feel wanting on Sunday mornings when my mother and sister donned their best dresses and my father, brother and I put on our freshly pressed suits and marched off as a family to Mass. We greeted our fellow parishioners gathered at the foot of

Special devotions at the Grotto of St. Eugene's chapel. This was an adjunct church which ministered to the over flow of parishioners from Sacred Heart church.

the gleaming white steps of the church with its large blue, red, yellow and green stained glass windows, the shining golden altar, and two side altars dedicated to the Blessed Mother and to St. Joseph. A huge, wooden crucifix hung from the high ceiling with Jesus, his hands nailed to the cross, his side pierced by a sword, and a crown of thorns piercing his bleeding head.

Our flourishing parish became the envy of neighboring pastors who referred to Sacred Heart Church as "Humphrey's Hilton" – after the grand hotel and our elderly and sometimes testy pastor, Monsignor William Humphrey, a convert to Catholicism.

In those days we were identified by the parish we lived in. When meeting another Catholic boy or girl in another part of the city we never asked, "Where do you live?" But rather, "What parish are you from?" St. Nicholas of Tolentine? Incarnation? Good Shepherd? Christ the King? Ascension? St. Jerome's? Holy Name? Our Lady of Perpetual Help? This was probably no different than when our Irish parents met another Irish person for the first time and asked, "And what county in Ireland are you from?"

When I grew up in the 1940's and 50's, Highbridge was a safe and predictable place where daily life held few surprises. The path awaiting a child as he entered Sacred Heart School was well-trod and tested by older brothers, sisters, cousins or neighbors who all blazed the same trail showing us the way.

Our teachers taught us that the United States of America was a Protestant country, but the only Protestants I knew were the Wyles family who were Glaswegian Presbyterians. Our Catholic world was separate with our own parochial schools, our Catholic School Athletic League, Catholic Youth Organization and quasi-Masonic Catholic men's lodges such as The Knights of Columbus and The Holy Name Society.

In the early 1990's after having moved away from the old neighborhood for almost 30 years, my sister, Mary, my brother, John, and I visited our old Sacred Heart School.

As a pale mid-morning sunlight filtered through the large classroom windows, my mind went back across a sea of years to another time – to Sister Mary Herbert, standing at the head of this very classroom where I now stood.

A Holy Communion

❧

The early spring of 1945. World War II is about to
end. Over fifty boys and girls cram together into
our second grade classroom. Sister Mary Herbert
stands tall at the front of the room in the black robes,
black veil and the white headband of a Sister of
Mercy. She announces: "Now that you are all seven
years old and have reached the age of reason, you
will be receiving your first Holy Communion. This
will be the happiest day of your life."

"Sister Mary Herbert is right," my mother nods
at dinner that night, "Holy Communion will be the
happiest day of your life." I look at my father. He
continues eating and says nothing.

The next day Sister points to a picture of St.
Patrick, a figure well known to us children of Irish
immigrants. "St. Patrick holds a shamrock." Sister
explains, "Although it has three leaves, it is just one
shamrock. The Holy Trinity contains three persons:
Father, Son and the Holy Ghost. All are one. All

are God. During communion you will receive the second person of the Trinity into your body in the form of a wafer called 'The Host.' This has been changed into the body and blood of the Son of God, Jesus Christ."

It sounds to me like the beginning of a fairy tale.

Later, my mother tells me it is all true and not made up. "It is a mystery," she says.

This is the first time I hear the word "mystery." In years to come, my young imagination will grapple with many other bewildering mysteries and rituals. I will learn to sing hymns in a foreign language called Latin: *Tantum Ergo, Salve Regina, Panis Angelicus*. I will have black ashes marked on my forehead by the priest on Ash Wednesday reminding me that from dust I come and to dust I shall return. On St. Blaise's Feast Day, my throat will be blessed with sacred candles. On Confirmation Day, my head will be anointed with holy oil by the Bishop who will lightly slap my cheek, then announce my new name – Augustine – and declare me a soldier for Christ. I will carry rosary beads and run my fingers through the five decades of beads reciting in unison with others: Hail Marys, Our Fathers and the Glory Be in honor of the Joyful, Sorrowful and Glorious mysteries. And then, at age 12, on the night of Holy Thursday, I will hold a lighted candle against the darkness of our church and join a procession of choir boys following the priest in his purple robes as he holds a silver crucifix on high. The fragrance of the incense as it rises in the air, the flickering light of the candles in the blackness, the hushed silence of the congregation broken only by the sound of our slow steps and steady chant of *Pange Lingua Gloriosi* – "Sing, my tongue, the Savior's Glory" – all this, on that night, will fire my young heart with a sense of awe, wonder and reverence I had never known before.

But that awaits me in the years ahead. Now I am only 7 years old trying to picture the happiest day of my life.

"Three rules you must remember," Sister says. "First, no eating or drinking on the morning of Holy Communion. Second, the host must never touch your teeth. Third, you must never, ever chew the Host."

Sacred Heart girls on their way to a devotional service. The art deco building behind them on the left is the Noonan Plaza once considered the most elegant apartment house in the borough.

A class of girls on their way to their first Holy Communion. Sacred Heart Church is in the background.

Second grade boys on their way to first Holy Communion. Sacred Heart School is in the background.

We boys prepare by trying on our very first suit
– navy blue with a white armband shaped like a
cross. We look like our fathers going off to church
on Sunday. The girls are even more excited with
their white lace dresses and veils, looking just like
their mothers in photographs taken on their parents'
wedding day.

Days before my First Holy Communion, I watch
tiny ants crawling on my window sill and I think
with wonderment, "God made even those tiny
ants. And He made the big tree across the street.
God made the great Yankee Stadium. He made
everything and everybody in the whole world. And
this great God almighty will be put on my tongue
and I will swallow Him into my stomach."

"A mystery," my mother says.

My legs shake as the Communion Mass begins.
We walk to the altar rail one row at a time as the
choir begins to sing, "O, Lord I am not worthy/
That Thou shouldst come to me."

Old Monsignor Humphrey pauses before each
kneeling child and speaking in Latin places the
wafer on each tongue. My stomach hurts and my
mouth is dry. "O, Lord I am not worthy... I am not
worthy."

I open my mouth, stick out my tongue, feel the
dry wafer and try to swallow it whole. I cannot. My
face is burning and I start to cough. "Take him away,"

Monsignor orders.

The altar boy holding a gold plate to catch even the slightest crumb of the sacred Host from falling to the ground, leads me away to the room beside the altar, the sacristy. Father Bond stands tall in his black cassock and with a slight smile on his face he pats my back. "C'mon, son, it's all right, take this water and swallow." Then, unbelievably, he says to me, "Go ahead, chew it!" I continue to cough as he leads me to the sink, "Here, spit it out!" I cough up the crumbled wafer and watch in horror as God Himself goes splattering into the sink, swirling down the drain like a potato peel I've seen in my mother's kitchen sink. Father Bond shrugs, slaps me lightly on the back, and says, "It's all right, go back to your seat."

Later my mother, father and I walk home in silence. Far from being the happiest day of my life, this has been the worst. As we are about to climb the stairs to our apartment, my father says, "Come with me, Mick." He takes my hand. His big hand is hard and rough as we walk down the long hill to the train station. Soon the two of us are sitting on the elevated subway going downtown to Manhattan.

"Where are we going?" I ask.

"To buy strings for my fiddle and resin for my bow," he smiles at me with a twinkle in his eye.

This is the very first time I ever remember being alone with my father, away from my mother, brother and sister. Is he angry with me about what happened at church? I study him. He himself is a "mystery" in a way. I know he comes from a place called Sligo, Ireland, which is across the Atlantic Ocean. I know he gets up each morning and goes to work on the IRT which is where most of my friends' Irish fathers work. And when he comes home from work each evening for dinner, he takes a nap, then goes off to another job as a night security watchman. When he returns home, we are all asleep.

As the train rumbles along, I recall the first time I asked my father about his fiddle. It was a hot summer's night and he was standing bare-chested by the kitchen window of our fifth floor apartment playing his violin. In those days before air conditioners, neighbors often sat by their windows hoping to catch a slight breeze amidst the broiling heat. On this particular evening neighbors found themselves listening to the sweet strains of my father playing Moonlight in Mayo drifting down from our open window to the courtyard below.

"Daddy, how did you learn to play the violin?" I ask.

In his Irish accent, my father says, "I play by air, Mick, by air."

Years went by before I realize he didn't just magically pull music out of the air. He meant, "By ear!"

The train stops at a station underground. My father leads me up the subway stairs toward the hot noisy streets of Manhattan. We come to a tiny store, "Mattie Haskins Irish Products."

My father greets the man behind the counter and with his hand on my shoulder, says, "This is my son, Mickey, he made his first communion today." With a big smile and in an accent like my father's, the man reaches out his big hand and says, "Well congratulations to you, my boy." Later my father buys me an ice cream cone and says, "I'm proud of you, son. Happy First Holy Communion Day."

With my hand still in his, we go home – my father less a mystery than before. I have learned something about him. The shame of that day has long since vanished; but what still lives inside me is the warm feel of my father's calloused hand, his knowing wink as we rode the train downtown to buy strings for his fiddle and resin for his bow, and the feeling deep inside that he was on my side and always would be. On that day I came to discover there is more than one kind of Holy Communion, and that Sister Mary Herbert – with her confident prediction – was not so far off when she promised it would be a very special day indeed.

Becoming a Yank

❧

In the late 1920's my mother and father abandoned the land of their birth because, in many ways, the land had abandoned them. Along with many thousands of others struggling on farms in rural Ireland, they sailed for America seeking a better life. Like the long wave of immigrants before and after them, they never completely abandoned their roots, and never stopped singing their Irish songs filled with nostalgic longing for the valleys, streams and meadows of their youth. But, over a period of time, their natural Irish gregariousness found an easy fit in the hustle and bustle of city life.

After my mother arrived in America, she brought over her younger brother, John, and her sister Margaret. My father brought over his younger sister, Amelia, and then his older brother, Pat. Some years later he sponsored his niece, Dolores McLoughlin. All of them, like my mother and father, eventually married, raised children and grandchildren and great-grand children of their own and became part of the great ongoing and unfolding story of America itself.

Like many immigrant families in America, our family had a foot in both worlds: Irish and American. My parents read two newspapers: *The Irish Echo* and *The New York Daily News.* Every March 17th they walked proudly up Fifth Avenue in the St. Patrick's Day parade. My father never missed his meetings of the Ancient Order of Hibernians, Division 9, and my mother was part of the Ladies Auxiliary. But no meeting was as important to my father as those of his trade union — the Transportation Workers of America. And on Election Day, going to the polls to vote the straight Democratic ticket was almost as sacred to Mom and Pop as going to Sunday Mass.

The Ancient Order of Hibernians, Division 9, was a major presence in our neighborhood. Here they parade through the streets on their way to a commemoration at the church.

Although they always remained "Irish to the backbone," my parents never stopped proclaiming how great America was. Of course, in those days of boundless optimism just after World War II, it was easy enough to be patriotic. America had just defeated Tojo in Japan and, once again, we rescued mighty Britannia – this time from the scourge of Nazism. And it did not go unnoticed in our family that many of those young soldiers who strapped rifles to their backs in World War II were born and bred Irishmen like our own uncle Frank McDermott who no sooner landed in New York in the 1930's from his small farm in County Cavan, than he was drafted into the United States Army to become an instant member of the "Greatest Generation." After his time in the U.S. Army, Uncle Frank needed no other proof that he was a full blown American.

To become a "full blown American "was a wish of my father as well. I recall an incident that brought home this wish to me.

One sweltering summer's night a year after the war ended, as I stood outside our apartment building, I noticed a huge glowing light flooding the dark sky. My mother explained that the brightness came from Yankee Stadium where they were holding the big prize fight. An Irish puncher from Pittsburgh named Billy Conn had come to town to challenge the great Joe Louis in an outdoor battle for the heavy weight boxing championship of the world.

In those school-boy days when sports were just about everything to us neighborhood kids, you got used to that kind of excitement and you came to expect that everything big and important happened just a few blocks away. Not only was the great Yankee Stadium nearby, but from my roof I could look across the Harlem River to see the outline of the mighty Polo Grounds where the New York Giants played baseball. It felt like living at the center of the universe.

Often on Saturdays, the owners of the New York Yankees handed out free grandstand tickets to us neighborhood kids. They dubbed us, "Yankee Juniors." But even when we couldn't get into the stadium for free, we happily paid the 60 cents to bake in the hot bleacher seats just to see the great DiMaggio play his last games as a Yankee. And later, in the early 1950's, when Mickey Mantle replaced the aging Joltin' Joe in center field, we packed the stadium and roared with the crowd as this new young lion smashed home runs and ran the bases in bullet speed no one had ever seen before. The New

York Yankees won four World Series in five years.

Baseball was the absolute king in our neighborhood. On summer weekends, platoons of fathers and sons marched through our local streets on their way to a ball game. On the streets right outside our apartment houses we kids played many variations of baseball: punch ball, curb ball, off-the-point and the king of all games, stickball – where we used a broom handle to hit a hard pink rubber ball, a spaldeen. The sewer covers were our bases.

Neither Mom nor Pop followed baseball, so I never went to a ball game with my father. Instead, on some Sundays after Mass, our parents took us on a rattling bus to the end of the Bronx to watch the Irish games at Croke Park. This was a sprawling place with a field – or a "pitch" as the Irish called it – and a restaurant bar owned by a big Kerry man, John O'Donnell. Later it became known as Gaelic Park.

With us kids in tow and amidst much banter, Mom and Pop joined their Irish friends in the sun-drenched, splintery stands to enjoy the national games of Ireland – Gaelic Football, a free-wheeling variation of soccer and rugby, and Hurling an all-out battle between two bands of swift warriors armed with wooden battle-axes, the hurley sticks.

"Up the field, Mayo!" "Up, Galway!" the crowd roared at the sound of the leathery smack of the stick against the ball. Out of pure "divilment" (as my mother would say) my father would cup his hands and chime in loudly amidst much laughter, "Up, DOWN! Up, DOWN!" – although I don't think County Down in the north of Ireland ever mounted a team of any kind in those days.

After the games, my parents and friends would stroll over for drinks at the huge, wrap-around bar followed by a dinner of ham and cabbage in the spacious dining room with a dance floor. Up on the stage, the likes of the ever-smiling Mickey Carton and his Irish band played waltzes, foxtrots, jigs and reels. People danced, songs were sung. It was a time for hard working New York Irish men and women to be among their own for a while, to share a few stories, trade news about the old country and have a few laughs before the new work week began on the morrow.

On these Sundays I took along my baseball and mitt hoping to find another Irish American boy dragged along by his parents to watch the Irish games. My new friend and I would play "catch" behind the stands, wishing we were watching the Yankees instead of being captive to the Irish "footballers" as Mom called them.

◈

Then on one particular Sunday we drove upstate
with other families from our parish for a picnic. In
the late afternoon a bunch of us boys chose up a
game of baseball and I was in the batter's box.

"C'mon," I shouted to the pitcher, "give me
something good to hit."

"One more strike and you're out!" he shouted
back.

I stepped back from home plate and saw a man
standing near first base. He was wearing a tan shirt
and trousers and leaning his arm against a tree.
He smiled as he watched me. It was my father. I
pretended not to see him. I stepped into the batter's
box determined to make him proud by slamming
that ball into the outfield. The next pitch came
sailing right down the middle of the plate and I
let go with the fiercest swing of my life. Damn! I
missed the ball again.

"Strike three. You're out!" the pitcher shouted
with glee.

I threw the bat to the ground and stole a look
down first base. My father stood gazing at me with
the same smile on his face as if I had just hit a home
run. He shrugged, winked and nodded as if to say,

"Attaboy, you show 'em!"
I had seen American fathers yell at their sons for
making even small mistakes on the baseball field.
My father must have known a swing and a miss was

not a good thing. His reaction puzzled me.

But then with the passage of years I came to realize something more about that day. As Irish-proud as he was, my father also wanted to be more "American." And I came to realize that a bridge to that American world for my father and for other Irish people I knew was often through their own children.

And so, as I recall the smile on his face that day, the approving wave of his hand, I see now it didn't matter to him whether or not I hit that baseball. What mattered was he had a son who was stepping up to the plate and becoming part of *the* game – the American way of things. That's what he wanted for himself – and what he most certainly wanted for his family.

Conflict On Tar Beach

❦

After the war, on summer nights, families in our neighborhood spent lots of time up on the roof. On August evenings, people in our five story apartment house gathered their beach chairs and climbed the stairs to the roof where they could enjoy a cool breeze off the river, away from the noise of the steamy streets below. We nicknamed our roof "tar beach." In those days before air conditioners and television, the roof was a gathering place where neighbors came together to chat about local politics or about who was having a baby or about some piece of news from the old country.

I am 9 years old, and it is another one of those humid nights. The women are sitting in a circle in their beach chairs on the roof after dinner. The sun is setting over Washington Heights across the Harlem River to the west. My mother in a sleeveless dress, her arms folded above her head, is holding forth to Mrs. Silver, Mrs. Kearney and Mrs. Wyles.

Some current news story has prompted a strange and controversial discussion.

"It is so clear to me what any mother should do in this case," my mother declares to the group, "A mother's duty is to her children, first and foremost."

No one joins in for several moments. Mrs. Kearney nods slightly in consent to Mom's words.

"It's a terrible and ridiculous choice," the dark haired Mrs. Silver says, "to have to choose between your husband or your children."

"Well, of course Mrs. Silver, we're not saying it's easy, but just suppose if you had a choice between your husband dying or your children, who would you choose? It's an easy one for me," my mother nods with conviction.

"Well I don't agree," Mrs. Wyles says. Jean Wyles is a small, pert woman, mother of two boys, my friends Roddy and Johnny. Her husband, Jimmy, is a tall, dark, muscular man from Glasgow. Like his wife, he had come to New York from Scotland in the early 1930's. Mrs. Wyles continues, "Oh God it would be hard to lose the children. I don't even want to talk about this terrible subject, but if it came down to it I just couldn't give up my Jimmy. No."

"But Jean," my mother insists, "Your children have their whole lives in front of them. Your husband has lived his life, the children still have so much to live for."

"I know you're right, but my Jimmy? No, I couldn't

let him go," Mrs. Wyles shakes her head apologetically.

The others stay silent. My mother leans forward like a politician trying to garner more local support. She continues, "Look. Let's face it, Jean, your children are your own flesh and blood. You gave birth to them. They must be protected. Oh, I know this is a most dreadful thing to be talking about, but it seems so obvious to me what the choice must be."

My mother never looks over at me the entire time. I sit off to the side just listening. What Mom says seems so logical and I am surprised when Mrs. Wyles quietly repeats, "I couldn't give up my Jimmy. He comes first." The more she says this, the more agitated my mother becomes.

"Your own flesh and blood, Jean!" She moves to the edge of her chair and leans into Jean Wyles who just sits there, her eyes downcast and says again, "I just couldn't."

I feel confused. My mother declares to these women that nothing is more important to her than her own children. That means me. But I cannot take my eyes off Mrs. Wyles slowly shaking her head looking to the ground, "I just couldn't give up my Jimmy." I feel a strange, puzzling, unexplainable admiration for this woman. I imagine a home where the father is king, the mother is queen, where all else flows from the fountain of their love, and the children are content to have it just that way.

Mamie and Gus

❦

My mother, Mary Ellen Gallagher, was the
oldest of five children of John Gallagher and
Catherine Clinton. She was born in a thatched
cottage in Boyney, County Leitrim on a small
farm not far from the resort town of Bundoran
in County Donegal. My mother's parents came
together in marriage through a match maker. John
Gallagher who owned some cows, chickens, and
pigs was a 47 year old bachelor in search of a wife.
Kate Clinton was an unmarried young woman
twenty years his junior who lived not far away in
County Leitrim in a place called Uragh near the
village of Kinlough. Kate was brought to Boyney to
meet John several times before the match was made
and a wedding date set. They married in 1910. The
following year on March 12, 1911, my mother was
born. Although christened Mary Ellen, she soon
became known as "Mamie" after a favorite aunt.

By the time my mother was 16 years old, her

*My mother's parents, John Gallagher and Catherine Clinton Gallagher
in County Leitrim, Ireland.*

parents decided she was old enough to leave home and make a better life for herself elsewhere. She had considered travelling to England as so many Irish country girls had done rather than have to cross the ocean, but she changed her mind when her two cousins, nurses in New Jersey, encouraged her to come to America.

In her later years she recalled that fateful day in 1927 when she stood on the quay in County Derry in the north of Ireland and bid farewell to her inconsolable parents. "What I remember most," she said, "was my mother could not stop crying." Perhaps her mother, Kate, who was then in her 40's, realized only too well what her departing teenage daughter did not: they might never lay eyes on one another again. Like so many thousands of others who left the west of Ireland in those years of the 1920's, the young left their homes, sailed for America, started families of their own and often could not afford to return.

Unlike my father who left Ireland as a 22 year old adventurous youth who enjoyed the singing and socializing as his ship sailed to New York, young Mamie Gallagher was a frightened girl, alone and seasick for her entire ocean voyage. Though only a teenager, she knew her journey carried a serious and important mission — to make money and send it back home. Never one to feel self pity throughout

My mother, Mary Ellen Gallagher Scanlon, known all her life as Mamie, just before she married my father.

her long life, she did confess in her later years to her teenage granddaughter, Jennifer, that she cried herself to sleep every night during that first year in America.

She came to New Jersey to become a nurse like her first cousins, Margaret and Katie Ruddy, who had arrived in America some years before. The two unmarried sisters worked at a hospital near Edgewater, New Jersey. As it happened, one of the patients at the hospital was a fellow Irish immigrant and the man who was to become my father.

My father was born May 6, 1906 in County Sligo, Ireland not far from the town of Ballisodare. His father, Michael, and his mother, Mary Ann McLean, produced nine children.

My father's parents, Michael Scanlon and
Mary Ann McLean Scanlon in County Sligo, Ireland.

Michael and Mary Ann with their son James who fought in World War I. Although as many as 49,000 Irish-born soldiers were killed in the war, Irish heroism in the war was sometimes marked by ambivalence back home in Ireland.

My father grew to be a short man, standing no more than 5'6", with a long name: Augustine Francis Aloysius Scanlon. He felt burdened by his "fancy" name and so became known simply as Gus. He determined his own three children should have simple, straight-forward names. And so it came to pass: we were John, Mary and Michael. My father called me "Mickey," a name that stuck with me throughout my youth. I called him "Pop" after a movie I had seen where an American kid called his father by that name, and that name stuck with him as well.

Only after 33 years when his family was grown did my father return to the "old country." I was his companion on that return trip in August of 1961. Pop was 55 years old and I was 22.

My father's sister, Ita, and her husband, Bertie Carroll, greeted us at the Dublin airport on that soft summer's day. We drove to their home, "Peacock House," a lovely two story white-stoned house with

My father, Augustine Francis Aloysius Scanlon known as Gus all his life.

a little greenhouse in the back garden in the town of Balbriggan outside Dublin.

As we sat at the kitchen table of Peacock House while my father slept, Aunt Ita explained why my father had pulled up stakes in his youth and left for America. Aunt Ita, a rosy-cheeked and cheery woman with a flair for the dramatic, stood over me serving up a fine breakfast of rashers, bangers and homemade toasted bread oozing with gobs of butter. She flipped two sizzling fried eggs onto my plate and then waving the kitchen spatula like an orchestra leader with his baton, she recounted: "Ah, well, your father, 'Gustin, was never the same after that day he came into that barn and discovered the dead body hanging from the rafters. That must have started him thinking it was time to get out. He was in his late teens by then."

I forget now who the person was that Pop saw hanging from the rafters. She continued, "But I think what really drove him to leave Ireland was the time the Black and Tans—those terrible British rowdies—came storming into our home one night and roused 'Gustin and our brother, Pat, out of their beds and dragged them down to the road to dig some sort of a ditch. They held guns over the lads' heads the whole time. Oh yes, I think that affected your father greatly. Not long after that, 'Gustin announced that he was going to America and, by

God, he did just that. He went off to New York and never came back until now."

Soon after he landed in New York City in 1928, Pop moved to Edgewater, New Jersey, the home of the Domino Sugar Factory, where he got his first job in America.

On a golden summer's afternoon almost a year after my father was released from the hospital in Edgewater after a short illness, he was walking down a leafy street and recognized the two Ruddy nurses who had attended him. With them was their young cousin, Mamie Gallagher, who had become a live-in domestic housekeeper for one Doctor Clarendon who owned a big, sprawling home in Hackensack, New Jersey. The gallant Gus tipped his hat to the ladies, and

My father and mother in their courting days.

then and there became smitten by young Mamie, five years his junior. On their first date, Gus took Mamie to Palisades Amusement Park. Years later my mother recalled, "From the first moment he picked me up until the last moment when we said good night, he had me laughing in stitches. I never had so much fun!"

They married on February 11, 1934 in St. Rose of Lima church on West 165th Street in Manhattan when he was 27 and she was 22. Mom's first cousin, Father Connell Clinton from Philadelphia presided. By this time my father had secured a job on New York City's IRT subway system as a power maintainer on the third rail. Mamie and Gus, like many of their fellow Irish immigrants, then moved to the West Bronx.

Seven years later they had three children: John Patrick, Michael Bernard, and Mary Patricia and we lived in a two bedroom apartment in a five story walk-up on a quiet and friendly street called Nelson Avenue, directly across from a Jewish synagogue.

In those days the wives and mothers in our neighborhood, most often stayed home and raised the kids, did the shopping, the cooking, the cleaning, the washing of clothes and the other tasks of homemaking.

During the week, my father awoke at 7am. He had a small breakfast of oatmeal and coffee which my mother made for him while he listened to the news and chat program, "Rambling with Gambling" on the radio. My mother packed sandwiches in a brown paper bag along with a thermos of tea. He left before 7:30 am, walked down the long public stairway to the train station on Jerome Avenue, arriving at his job on the Interboro Rapid Transit

(I.R.T.) at 8 am. He left work at 4 o'clock returning home before 5. Often on his way home, after climbing back up the steep stairway to our neighborhood on the hill, he paid a brief visit at Sacred Heart church. I used to wonder what he prayed for on those visits. When asked, Mom quietly replied, "He does it for a special intention." I never learned what that intention was.

His dinner waited for him in our little kitchen. Dinner was preceded by his version of the cocktail hour: a shot of rye whiskey followed by a can of Ballantine beer as a chaser. He called it "a ball and a beer," more commonly known as a "boiler maker." After dinner he sat in his yellow upholstered chair reading his Daily News before climbing into bed for a nap, only to wake up an hour later for his second job.

Before going off, he joined in the family's reciting of the rosary. "A family that prays together, stays together," an Irish priest named Father Peyton from County Mayo had preached to various parishes throughout New York City during the early 1950's, and so it was that my mother deemed it proper that a nightly rosary be recited by our family. Each of us gathered in the living room kneeling at a different corner of the room near a chair we could lean on. We recited the five decades of the rosary. My father, just roused from sleep and thinking of the long night ahead of him, was most somber and serious during this ritual.

The rosary completed, Pop left for his second job as a security watchman. When he arrived home after midnight, our family was asleep. The next morning he began the same routine all over again. Many years later, as my brother John and I sipped tea in John's opulent apartment on the upper west side of Manhattan, he said, "I think Daddy may have been the hardest working man I ever knew."

On nights when he did not go to the second job, Pop rolled his own cigarettes. He had a formal procedure. He pulled a straight back chair in front of him and used the chair's seat as his little work bench. Folding loose tobacco from the packet of "Bugler Tobacco" into the sleeve of his little cigarette-making machine, he licked the cigarette paper and placed it in the machine and with a flick of the wrist he'd roll a "ready-made." With a scissors he cut off the loose ends of tobacco protruding from each end of the cigarette and placed his 20 cigarettes in a small plastic container the size of a real pack of cigarettes. His cigarettes always came out thinner than a regular cigarette and were quite mild to smoke.

One time when he and Mom accompanied me and my wife, Rosemary, to visit my wife's family in Nova Scotia, he packed a large supply of his "roll-your-own" cigarettes into several clear plastic bags. When we arrived in Canada, he was made to open his suitcase for a customs check, and the young Canadian custom official noted all these thinly rolled cigarettes. He pulled them out suspiciously and held them up in front of Pop's face and in an accusatory tone demanded, "And what, may I ask, are these, sir?"

I stood off to the side and witnessed my poor Irish father being suspected of smuggling marijuana. Pop, of course, had no idea why he was being questioned and answered with surprise, "Well, those are my cigarettes." The official turned to his supervisor nearby. The supervisor, an older and obviously wiser fellow than his earnest young charge, recognized Pop's innocence at once and nodded to the young official to let Pop go free with his Glad bag of cigarettes. Pop, having no clue as to what had just transpired, leaned towards Mom after they were out of earshot of the customs men and whispered, "You'd think that young fella never saw a cigarette in his life!"

My father was a passionate supporter of his union, *The Transport Workers Union*. When he first went to work for the IRT in the early 1930's, it was

privately owned and non-union. Like many of his
fellow workers, he worked 12 hours a day, 7 days a
week for 33 cents an hour. In theory, he was entitled
to two days off without pay each month. But if he
requested these "entitled" days two months in a row,
he would be ordered to the medical department for
a check-up, and if he requested them again the next
month, the IRT medical department would find
him "unfit for duty." He could be fired. He saw it
happen to others.

When a fellow worker at the IRT, Mike Quill
from County Kerry, began organizing the men
to correct these injustices, my father was one of
the first to join. Organizing the union was a long,
hard-fought battle, but the cause was right and
just and – after many a broken head – the union
won out. It freed my father and his fellow workers
from hardship conditions and gave them a sense
of respect and a living wage to raise a family. The
union and Mike Quill were as sacred in our home
as the Church and the Pope.

Quill was a fire-brand leader who had been
an Irish rebel back home in Ireland during "the
troubles," and he brought with him to New York
City shrewd talents for organizing men which
he had learned in the I.R.A. He was forever
threatening strikes of the entire New York transit
system.

A reporter once asked him if he thought Mayor Robert Wagner, was a "spineless" individual, to which Quill replied, "Well, I am not an orthopedic surgeon so I cannot comment on the state of the man's spine!" With his heavy, Irish brogue he brought delight to us American kids of Irish descent and our parents enjoyed hearing us do take-offs of him. Quill most famously declared, "The Bible says the meek shall inherit the earth, But I say to ye the meek shall inherit nuttin'!" Make fun of him as we would, Mike Quill "brought home the bacon" and was a hero to his union members and most certainly to my father.

Daily Life

❖

The monthly rent on our two bedroom apartment was $53.00. Yet growing up in Highbridge we never felt poor. We ate very well with delicious roast chicken, or leg of lamb or big hams served up every Saturday night, our main meal of the week. That meal was often preceded by a whole day spent at the Crest or Ogden Movie Theatres where admission was 25 cents for those over 12 years old and 12 cents for those under 12. Many of us 13 or 14 year olds would bend our knees to appear younger to get the cheaper rate. For those 12 cents we got to see two full length features plus cartoons and "This Week in News and Sports." On those Saturdays we were transported into new worlds by tough guys like James Cagney, Humphrey Bogart, Allan Ladd or Edward G. Robinson in gangster movies, or Fred Astaire, Gene Kelly and Frank Sinatra in musicals, or big John Wayne, Henry Fonda and James Stewart in Westerns.

With empty stomachs we would come home to the delicious and mouth-watering smells of my mother's kitchen and my father saying as we gathered around the kitchen table, "Who wants more blood from the roast beef?" and me clamoring as I held up my plate practically wiped clean from my licking it all up, "Me, me, Daddy, I love the blood." And he'd pour the juices from the roast beef onto my plate and I'd sop it all up with the fresh rye bread filled with caraway seeds from the local Jewish bakery on 168th Street.

Few activities my mother enjoyed more than that of hostess of a dinner party or any kind of get-together of friends and family. She joyed in bringing people together, serving them their favorite cocktail, providing plentiful food and making connections between one person and another.

Once seated at a table heavy with all manner of meats, potatoes and vegetables, one of the guests would invariably say, "Ah, Mamie, will you ever sit down and join us and stop your running around taking care of everyone else?" And Mom would reply as she served up yet another dish of vegetables, "Ah well, I like it this way. Let you all just sit back and enjoy yourselves and I'll take care of myself, don't you worry. Here, Jimmy, let me refill your glass while I'm at it, and I have creamed onions coming up so leave some room."

About every six months or so my mother discovered a new wallpaper she could not live without. Paint and turpentine became a recurring smell around our little home. Up would go the ladders and Mom climbing them, the better to rip off the old and slap on the new. Baseboards were painted afresh, floors shellacked, furniture moved. Indeed, often when finished, she would decide to make the bedroom into the living room and vice-versa. She was ever in search of getting it just right.

This was brought home to me that most memorable day in 1952 when we brought home our first television set. Finally we kids wouldn't have to pile into someone else's apartment to watch "Howdy Doody" (whom I never particularly liked myself). Most people in the neighborhood in the early 1950's bought television sets that stood in the middle of the living room like a big cyclopean gray eye staring out at you the minute you walked into the room. Not for Mom. For her it was not the television that was as important as the decorative wooden cabinet it came in. Televisions in those days were usually Philcos, Admirals, Zeniths or the one we chose: Emerson with a 13 inch screen. Our television stood inside a lovely beige cabinet with two doors and carved handles so the big gray eye was never seen until you turned the TV on.

Even as a 12-year-old boy I knew our television set looked better than any other set I had ever seen. I knew this just as I knew we had the prettiest drapes in our living room, the nicest couches and chairs, the loveliest bedspreads on our beds. That was all Mom — the poor country girl from Ireland who seemed born with the decorating touch and an instinctive taste for "better things."

Outside of school we mixed and played sports with the Jewish kids who made up the other half of our neighborhood. And while they were taught they were the "chosen people," we were taught the same about ourselves. Priests and our Catholic school teachers never ceased reminding us that we were the truly "chosen": "Unless you are baptized in the blood of Jesus Christ you cannot be saved. Only through the Catholic Church will you reach salvation."

The Second World War broke out in September of 1939 when I was three months old. All during my pre-school years I constantly heard the name Hitler. With his ugly voice and his tiny little mustache and slicked down hair, he seemed a ridiculous figure to us kids. We made fun of him by putting our index finger under our noses pretending to have a mustache and raised our arm in salute and shouted, "Heil Hitler!" My mother yelled at me to stop doing that. Of course, at my age I did not understand what Hitler had to do with the Jewish people. We would light fires and put a stick on the pile of burning branches and shout, "That's Hitler. Let's watch the fire creep up on him and burn him to death – Burn! Burn! Burn!

Our apartment faced directly across the street from the neighborhood synagogue, the "Shul," built in 1936. I recall many an early Saturday morning looking out from our fifth story bedroom window with my sister, Mary, as the two of us absorbed the quietude and peacefulness of Nelson Avenue. We watched as fathers with their sons went to synagogue on those Sabbath mornings — Jews carrying prayer books not unlike myself during a piety phase of my early teens when I walked up that same avenue on quiet weekday mornings with my missal in hand on my way to the 7:15 am daily Mass at Sacred Heart Church.

The synagogue still stands today with a Star of David emblazoned in a stained glass window above the front door, but now it houses a Christian Pentecostal church.

I was recruited by Mr. Marcus on Friday evenings to turn off the lights in the synagogue. Only years later did I learn they had a term for me: "shabbos goy." Once inside the synagogue, I took note of the spotless pews and stained glass windows. In the front, instead of the commanding pulpit of our church, there stood a simple lectern in front of the altar with wooden carved doors. In its tranquility and stillness it felt like our church except it was smaller, and there were no statues.

Mr. Marcus, a quiet man with a kindly but mournful demeanor, wore the toe of one of his shoes cut open so that his white sock showed. Later, someone told me he suffered from the gout. He would say to me, "Close the light," a locution not familiar in my home where we simply said, "Shut off the light." He had me climb up on a shelf where a large panel of switches was mounted on the wall and he would say, "Close that one. Not that one, the other one. Okay, now close that one." Because the panel was hard to reach I assumed at first this was why he brought me to perform this task. Only when we stood together just inches from a light switch and he pointed, "Close that one" did I realize that this business of switching off lights had something to do with a religious rite. To a Catholic boy like myself, this Jewish ritual about "closing the lights" on Fridays seemed rather odd, except it was not any more odd than my being forbidden to eat meat on Fridays or having to go into a tiny dark booth, the confessional, to tell my sins to a priest on Saturday afternoons.

For me the best part about church-going was always the music. Unlike today where the whole congregation joins in song at Mass, in the 1940's and 50's only the boys' choir sang. Rather than choosing to be altar boys, my brother John and I joined the choir. And though we may not have understood the meaning of *Laudamus, Adoramus or Glorificamus* at the time, the ancient Latin songs added magical rhythm to the mysterious atmosphere of the lighted candles on the altar and colorful vestments on the priests. To this day when I find myself part of a congregation of worshippers – whether Jewish, Catholic or Protestant – and the whole flock lifts its voice loudly and joyfully in unison, I feel a sense of awe and brotherhood and am more easily inspired to believe in a transcending power greater than myself. St. Augustine had it right when he wrote: "To sing is to pray twice."

A Corner of My Home

A cold winter's morning. I am 8 years old and bring the "Funnies Section" of the Sunday Daily News into bed. Here is Dick Tracy with his bright yellow fedora and yellow overcoat driving along a deserted road searching for his prey. The caption reads: "A blanket of snow covers the ground as Dick drives into the frosty country side." I think to myself, "Wow, a blanket of snow covering the ground—just as my smooth white blanket covers me now in my warm bed on this freezing Sunday morning in New York City." I love the way "blanket" and "snow" go together. Later on, I feel the same pleasant sensation when a classmate writes about a blue sky with "pink powder puff clouds." I think of my mother's soft powder puff. It is the first time I am aware of language casting a spell and the beginning of my love for poetry, metaphor and imagination.

Comic books were the only books I read in those days. I gazed for hours at the colorful pictures

and the little bubbles above the heads of Captain
Marvel, Batman, Superman, Terry and the Pirates,
Captain America, The Phantom, or Archie and his
friends Jughead along with the pretty blond-headed
Betty and the dark haired Veronica (my favorite).
And then there were the "classic" comics featuring
Ivanhoe, Don Quixote, The Deerslayer, and my
favorite, Robinson Crusoe – one man struggling
to survive on a desert island with his parrot and his
man "Friday." I felt the same thrill reading The Swiss
Family Robinson as a shipwrecked family, alone on
an island, devises ways to stay alive in the jungle.

Many a day I even curled up with a pile of
"romance" comics by my side in which Pamela
pined for Brad while Brad pined for Deborah and
they were shown kissing and calling each other,
"Darling" and I wondered if one day I would kiss
the big red lips of someone as pretty as Deborah
and have her call me, "Darling."

In those days before television we traded stacks of
comic books with our friends. World War II comic
books proliferated at that time where our American
G.I. Joe heroes, covered in mud, blasted their rifles
and threw hand grenades at the dreaded German
or Japanese enemy. They inspired me and my
cousin, Vincent Gallagher, to draw our own pictures
sketching all the blood and gore found in these war
comics. In school we had a proper class called "Art"

taught by an eccentric but likeable woman named Miss Hersey. Airplanes became my favorites to draw in that class; horses were the toughest.

The quiet of mind, the deep engagement of imagination, the contentment of aloneness with a book—even a comic book—these took root in me.

Other than our school books, the only books I remember in our home were an encyclopedia set kept in a small bookcase near our kitchen. There must have been 15 to 20 thin volumes. I cannot recall anyone ever reading them.

Over that book case hung a framed picture of Jean-Francois Millet's *The Angelus*, depicting two peasants, a woman and a man, standing in a potato field. The man holds his beret to his chest, his head is bowed with a deep feeling of respect. The woman too bows her head and joins her hands up close to her face. Nearby, a sack of potatoes sits on a wooden wheel barrow. Years later as I studied the original painting in the Musee d'Orsay in Paris, I felt an immense sense of the eternal in the painting. But as a boy I had no idea the couple was taking a moment to meditate as the bell tolled for the mid-day prayer. I only remember feeling a little sad as I looked at that picture with its brown tones – as if the woman and man were mourning something I didn't understand. Of all the prints my mother could have chosen, I wonder why she picked this

one to hang in such a prominent place in our home.
Was it the prayerful reverence of the two peasants?
Or did the picture remind her of her home and
family left behind in Ireland?

Culture in our home did not consist of visiting
museums or going to the opera or Broadway shows.
It touched on the love of "the song." My mother's
favorites were "Those Two Eyes of Blue," "The
Whistling Gypsy," and "Galway Bay." Many of the
songs we heard as children were long, mournful
ballads that told stories, like the one my mother
often sang of the Irish country lad who falls
madly in love with the beautiful Annie only to be
wrenched from her arms by the cursed English army
which sends him off to fight in the Napoleonic Wars.
A long time passes as the young lovers yearn for
each other. Fearing her lover has died, the dejected
and broken-hearted Annie takes to her bed just as
the young soldier boy flees the English army, fights
his way back to Ireland, and finally arrives at Annie's
door. My mother always took a pause at this point
in the ballad, letting the room fill with hushed
suspense before she sang the fateful and final words
of the song: "*And he found she was dead!*" A gasp, and
then inevitably someone in the room, after taking
a long drag on a cigarette, would mutter, "Ah lovely,
Mamie, just lovely! God bless ya."

With the Irish — I came to realize fairly early on — the sadder, the better! Especially when it came to love and patriotism. Blood and guts, martyrdom and death — the Irish could not get enough of it. G. K. Chesterton summed it up best when he wrote:

> *The great Gaels of Ireland are the men*
> *that God made mad,*
> *For all their wars are merry, and*
> *all their songs are sad.*

One of the best singers was my mother's sister, Aunt Margaret. Arriving in America in 1939 she became known among her crowd of "greenhorns" for her pleasing soprano voice. A friend submitted her name to the popular national radio show The Major Boes Amateur Hour. She was assigned an American Irish tin-pan alley song, I'm Off To Philadelphia in the Morning – a song she had never heard of; but she mastered it in time for the live radio performance and succeeded in taking second prize.

Shortly after her radio "debut," a letter arrived from Palm Beach, Florida from a woman inquiring whether Aunt Margaret would be interested in the position of *au pair* for her youngest child. Margaret consulted my mother who advised against going too far from New York City where young Margaret had her only family in America. The letter writer said she was the mother of ten children and the child in question was her 7 year old boy, Teddy. She signed her name: Rose Kennedy. This was a long before the Kennedy name became famous. One is now left to wonder how Teddy Kennedy would have turned out were he to have been serenaded as a little boy by the sweet, dulcet tones of Maggie Gallagher from County Leitrim, Ireland.

My mother was asked to sing at many public events.

When my father wasn't entertaining with his fiddle playing, he could sing a limitless number of Irish songs.

My father sang all manner of songs: the merry and the sad, songs of courtship, of maternal love, of the beauty of the land, of home sickness as well as good old fashioned Irish and American patriotic songs. And on special occasions he even recited a favorite American poem, The Face On The Barroom Floor. One night, towards the end of a party I heard someone say, "Ah shure, with Gus it's like Jesus with the loaves and fishes, the more he sings the more another one pops up in his head." Once at Gaelic Park after the Irish games, my father stood at the bar and was asked to sing one song after the other by his friends. With each new song they stood him another drink. The following day I said to him, "Boy, Pop, you sure are popular among your friends. They all gathered around to hear you sing." And he turned to me with a slight twinkle in his bleary eyes and replied, "Well, Mick, have you ever heard of the fella who was just too popular for his own good?" My mother, within earshot, slowly nodded in agreement.

My mother had her own favorite poet of light verse: Edgar Guest. I recall evenings in our pre-TV living room when Mom would recite for us Eddie Guest's latest from the Journal American newspaper. The following lines must surely have resonated with her own life:

When you're up against a trouble,
Meet it squarely, face to face;
Lift your chin and set your shoulders,
Plant your feet and take a brace.
When it's vain to try to dodge it,
Do the best that you can do;
You may fail, but you may conquer,
See it through!

Guest's sentimental, optimistic poems were scoffed at by the sophisticated Algonquin set, but he was loved by millions. He wrote over 20 books of poetry, was syndicated in over 300 newspapers throughout the country, and was known as the "People's Poet."

As simple and sometimes corny as these songs and light verse poems may have been, our parents were teaching us children about the comforting pleasure of rhyme and metaphor. In years to come, with education, we would learn to appreciate the masters like Shakespeare, Yeats and Joyce, but in our home the seeds for appreciation of story and language were first planted in us at the feet of our Irish parents.

In our little foyer for as long as I can remember, we had a piano. Mom herself started lessons with Mrs. Simmons up on Miriam Avenue, and I can still see her sitting upright at the piano in the evening in her black dress with little white polka-dots trying to master the lovely song "Beautiful Heaven," a translation from the great Spanish classic, "Cielto Lindo." It wasn't long before she realized that taking piano lessons and raising us three children were too much, so she reluctantly gave it up. My older brother, Johnny, was next in line for lessons. He hated every minute of it.

There is hardly is an experience more frightening to a child than seeing a parent cry. My mother cried when she discovered Johnny had kept the money for his piano lesson and had instead bought candy for himself. Mom confronted him and wept, "How could you do such a selfish thing, Johnny?" My skinny, blond, curly-headed older brother just stood there saying nothing. I remember thinking Johnny had a boldness and daring about him that I could not muster. In spite of the pain he caused, I had a strange admiration for his taking what he wanted for himself, consequences be-damned. Early on Johnny possessed an inborn audacity, a fearlessness which he developed later in life, often yielding great beneficial results for himself as he rose in the business world to become one of the nation's top public relations gurus.

After Johnny stopped piano lessons, I began. Off I

went to Mrs. Simmons, a thin dried-skinned proper woman, who taught scales and old classics like "Beautiful Dreamer" by Stephen Foster. That was the one song I mastered, but, alas, like my older brother, I soon tired of practicing the piano since it robbed me from playing stick ball down on the street with my friends.

Now as I reflect on that piano, and that Millet print of The Angelus and that set of encyclopedia in its neat little book case, I know these were there because of my mother. It was she who always made the effort and was ever in search of ways to uplift our little home.

Johnny Leaves Home

—◆—

I'm a little teapot, short and stout
Here is my handle, here is my spout
When I get all filled up, don't you doubt
Tip me over, and pour me out.

My brother had to learn this song in second grade, and I will never forget my mother standing in the living room showing him over and over again how to sing this little ditty. She wanted him to get it just right for his class performance. She demonstrated the gestures: one arm making a half circle for the handle, the other arm held up and bent to be the spout. She then tipped her body sideways as she sweetly sang the final words, "Tip me over and pour me out!" My plump mother looked very much like the perfect little tea kettle.

I sat off on the side listening to this song I had never heard before and finding it so pleasingly melodic and delightful.

Whatever Johnny did, I wanted to do. He started a stamp collection which was so popular among children in those days, so I started one too. He had a big brown covered book, and I had a little blue covered book. I recall those ancient evenings just after World War II when the family gathered around the radio listening to Jack Benny with Johnny and me in the middle of the floor with our stamp books while my sister, Mary, sat quietly on my mother's or father's lap – the pretty little blond baby girl adored by both parents. She was named 'Mary' after my mother and, of course, after Mary, the mother of Jesus.

My mother was very religious. In our local Catholic school the boys were taught by brothers belonging to a French order founded by St. Jean Baptiste de la Salle in the 18th century. These Brothers were clean-cut men which recommended them highly to my mother whose highest compliment about any man was, "He's so clean-cut!"

Although my mother paid all due respect to the priests, she recognized that the brothers, as well as the nuns, were the worker bees of the parish. The brothers taught us boys both religious subjects and academic school subjects, and coached us in track, basketball and football.

When Johnny graduated from Sacred Heart School, at age 13, he announced he wanted to become a Christian Brother. This meant he would go away to a high school in upstate New York which would prepare him before he took the vows of poverty, chastity and obedience and donned the robes of a religious brother.

The day he left our little home, September 2, 1948, is a day emblazoned in my memory. Mom, Johnny and my 9 year old self walked sadly down Nelson Avenue on a gleaming late summer's day to 166th street and made the right turn onto Ogden Avenue where we met a group of boys from the parish also going away to become brothers. The boys bid farewell to their parents, boarded a bus to Grand Central Station where a train would take them upstate to Barrytown about 100 miles from the city on the Hudson River.

That day, the constellation of our family changed forever. Johnny left us and never came back except for a brief two week vacation every summer, but it was never, ever the same. He was gone.

I don't recall my mother shedding tears the day Johnny left. She hardly spoke to me when we walked home after hugging and kissing him goodbye. Years later I would learn the meaning of the word "stoic" and I thought of Mom on that day. Was she thinking about her own 16 year old self who parted from her mother and father only 20 years before and had never seen them since? What went through her mind I cannot tell, but I know some part of her must have been proud, no doubt, that a child of hers wanted to devote his life to God.

Two Sundays throughout the year, our family of four took the train or boarded a big clattering

My mother and brother John just after he donned the robe of a Christian Brother in Barrytown, New York.

The Scanlon family at Barrytown, New York in 1952.

Visiting Johnny when he was on summer break from college in Oakdale, New York.

bus heading up route 9 to St. Joseph's High School where the boys were taught religious studies along with their regular high school subjects.

Those visits to Barrytown were happy Sundays indeed. The school sat in the midst of country fields and had baseball diamonds and two gyms. Johnny seemed to thrive there. He put on much needed weight and he saw himself, rightfully so, as the shining star of our family. He was taken care of by those smiling, celibate "clean cut" men who were devoted to God's work. We knew one day Johnny himself would put on the black robe and white collar of a brother and go out into the Catholic schools of New York and teach boys their school subjects and how to become good Catholics.

I recall a vivid memory from one of those Sundays when we visited Johnny in Barrytown.

After our day of visiting is over, we board a train to return home. Mom, Pop, Mary and I wave goodbye to Johnny who stands on the platform with all the other boys waving goodbye to their parents. Then, as our train slowly pulls away from the station, Johnny breaks out of the pack and starts jogging alongside our departing train and shouting "Good-bye, good-bye, good-bye." The rest of the boys remain on the platform of the station. As the train picks up speed, Johnny picks up speed. He runs past the platform and scampers onto the dirt path beside the train tracks trying to keep up, running as fast as he can, waving all the time and shouting "Goodbye, good-bye!" I keep yelling back, "Goodbye Johnny, goodbye" until finally the train pulls so far ahead of him that he stops and just stands there dropping his arms to his side until little by little he becomes a tiny dot in the purple twilight as our train roars its way back to New York City.

I wish now I could remember the look on my mother's and father's face as this happens. So many good-byes in their lives. So many separations from parents and siblings. Both of them certainly knew what it felt like to be young and leaving a family behind. And now this, their oldest child—13 years old—living 100 miles away from his family and coming home briefly only once a year.

I have never been sure how my father felt about his son devoting himself to the religious life.

Past Meets Present

Every summer my father got a few weeks
vacation from the IRT and we headed down
to Rockaway Beach, "The Irish Riviera." Like
many other Irish American families from the
neighborhoods of Inwood or Washington Heights
in Manhattan, or Woodside and Sunnyside in
Queens, or Bay Ridge in Brooklyn, the Scanlon
family trekked from the Bronx to rent two rooms at
a boarding house for three weeks.

One hot evening in the late 1940's when I was
7 or 8 Mom and Pop took me along with them to
that rollicking block of 103rd Street in Rockaway
Beach called "Irish Town." One Irish bar attached to
another on both sides of the sprawling street. Fiddle
and accordion music – with a mixture of America's
top hits – spilled out from the bars onto the cheery
and carefree streets. Men and women, freshly
sunburned from the day at the beach, strolled from
one bar to the other with glasses in hand. It was like

the Wild West saloons I had seen in movies. I most vividly recall The Sligo House and The Leitrim Hotel, the two home counties of my parents, which faced each other on opposite sides of the street.

My father held my hand as we entered a big noisy bar with a huge circular stage which took up almost the entire room. "Ah, look at them, Gus," my mother said with a wide smile as she poked my father, "Up on the stage, it's the McNulty family!" And here was Mrs. McNulty, an older woman all powdery and shining, sitting on a chair playing the accordion, while her grown daughter and son in top hats and tails sang and tap danced to the song,

> *Johnny get up from the fire, get up*
> *and give the man a seat*
> *Don't you see it's Mr. McGuire and*
> *he's courtin' your sister Kate*
> *You know very well he owns a farm a*
> *wee bit out of the town*
> *So get up out of there and be takin' the*
> *air and let Mr. McGuire sit down!*

Irish Town provided a great summer refuge from the hot tenements of pre-air conditioned New York City. And if spending nights taking in the sights and sounds of Irish town wasn't enough, Playland was

nearby on 98th street, a small amusement park like
Coney Island with the sweet smell of cotton candy,
the hot dogs, the penny arcade, a shooting gallery,
a roller coaster, and most especially the "bumper
cars." Sometimes when I am near a beach and take
in that first smell of sea air I am instantly, almost
mysteriously, thrown back to those days when I was
young in Rockaway Beach.

As teenagers we rode the ocean waves, played
"dog ball" on the beach – another form of baseball.
On some afternoons we would stop by the Beach
108th street playground and watch local Rockaway
men, the brothers Dick and Al McGuire – both
New York Knickerbockers – play basketball. At night
we went to Mamey's ice cream parlor, straight out
of a Norman Rockwell painting and a far cry from
the tiny candy stores we had back in Highbridge.
We held parties among the boys and girls. For a boy
like myself who was educated in classrooms from
the third grade on filled only with boys, it was a
refreshing treat to finally break out and socialize
more closely with girls my age. And so it happened
in the summer of 1954 that I became utterly smitten
and besotted with one Patty Cassidy – who I saw as
a golden blond, freckled-faced, pony-tailed Bronx
Irish Catholic goddess!

Our family was staying at Frain's rooming house
at 113th Street at Rockaway Beach. I was 15. Patty

and her Irish parents were staying at a boarding house across the street. Along with a large group of other boys and girls our age we played on the beach, went to the ice cream parlor at night; I made jokes, she laughed, we took bike rides together and the closest I ever got to kissing her was at a party when we all played "Spin the Bottle." I remember listening to that Nat King Cole song which was popular at the time:

> They tried to tell us we're too young,
> Too young to really fall in love,
> They say that love's a word,
> A word we've only heard
> And can't begin to know the meaning of.

"At least someone understands," I pined. Then much later, I read James Joyce's short story "Araby" from *The Dubliners* and was astonished that Joyce should know how I felt when I was fifteen and under a mysterious spell I could hardly understand. Joyce wrote, "At night in my bedroom and by day in the classroom her image came between me and the page I strove to read ... I did not know whether I ... could tell her of my confused adoration."

Patty was a flirt and, with her shining blond hair, she was popular with the boys on the beach. After that magical summer ended, we wrote letters for a while and then drifted apart. Still, I carried a photo of her for a long time and I never forgot her sassy, lively self.

Then twenty years after the summer we met, we met again by chance on the boardwalk of Rockaway Beach very near the place I first laid eyes on her. Her parents, like mine, had moved to Rockaway Beach (Belle Harbor) during the late 1960's and Patty was visiting her parents as I was visiting mine. It was a chilly, foggy day in early December as I tossed a football with my nine year-old son, Sean. The boardwalk was empty and suddenly out of the fog I see Patty Cassidy walking towards me.

She had married with two children and was now divorced. I watch as she takes out a cigarette, lights it with a little gold lighter and inhales deeply. Her once golden hair is now brown with dyed streaks of blond and a tooth is missing. Her eyes are watery. A weariness comes off her. As we sit on a bench on the boardwalk with the cold wind sweeping in from the sea, we have little to say. We live in two different worlds. She finishes her cigarette, steps on it, smiles a little sadly, says goodbye and goes on her way up the boardwalk. We never saw one another again.

—◆—

How many awkward moments have I spent
meeting close childhood friends in later years
realizing we have nothing to say to one another.
"Is this the same person I shared so many close
and intimate moments with?" I ask myself. How
many books have I loved when young only to be
unmoved by them later in life? How many movies
stirred me to laughter or tears only to leave me
cold when I see them as an adult? And how many
times did I recall my old dear neighborhood of
Highbridge as it used to be in the old days – and
what it had become?

On a rare visit to the old neighborhood I came
away with a heavy heart. The sense of village
had vanished. Apartment houses on Woodycrest
Avenue that used to sing with the life of bustling
Irish families had become burnt-out tombs.
The neighborhood library on Shakespeare Avenue
was sealed over like a war torn bunker with
protective fences. And, although our church of
Sacred Heart still stood like a mighty fortress in
faded white splendor, it was now locked shut after
morning Mass.

Most of the sons and daughters of the Irish who
had settled in Highbridge before and after World
War II had left by the early 1970's. Even as early as
first grade of school when reading about "Dick and
Jane" in our little reading books, we Highbridge

kids knew a better world awaited us beyond the borders of the old neighborhood. That was the world of neat, little quiet homes with a garage, green lawns, picket fences and a big friendly, fluffy dog. As we grew, the urge to move out and move up followed. For some that meant finding a new home in the suburbs, for others it meant finding bigger apartments in better neighborhoods. I moved out in 1962 to join the United States Navy and never came back.

As we departed, the new immigrants from the Dominican Republic, Puerto Rico, Africa, the West Indies, and Blacks from the South came seeking the same passage to America that our parents had sought a generation before. But the 1960's and 70's were a time when the epidemic of drugs took root and infested neighborhoods all over the city. Highbridge was hit especially hard by the scourge of heroin and crack, and by the late '70's, the 44th police precinct registered the highest crime rate in the city.

As dismaying as this was, Highbridge still owned a part of me I could not fully explain. An urge to somehow reclaim my early years had stirred quietly inside me. And so – after a 35 year absence – I did come back. I became an English teacher at Bronx Community College located on the old New York University campus, blocks away from where

I once lived.

I left the community as a son of immigrants and then came full circle to return as an older teacher to the new immigrants. Along the way I discovered the truth of the old adage: You can never really go home again. But I also learned that in spite of all the changes and differences between the past and the present, some things remained the same. While visiting Sacred Heart Grammar School I found it was as clean and orderly as the day I left. It had survived as a community sanctuary – the single shining example of constancy and stability amid the blight and decay of the surrounding neighborhood. Inside, the walls were unmarked, the brightly colored classrooms as organized as I remembered them. The smiling, alert boys and girls were dressed in neat maroon and white uniforms. Many of these grade schoolers were not Catholic, most of them Hispanic or African American, and yet I saw myself in them.

In the course of the ten years I taught at Bronx Community College I came to realize this little corner of the Bronx was just another manifestation of the long and changing and unfolding story of America itself.

Leocadia Rodriguez, a student of mine, age 28, lives on the same block where I was born and raised. She writes about the day she arrived alone in America from the Dominican Republic as a 16-year-old girl, hopeful one day to become a nurse but fearful about her prospects. I read this and see my own mother who also arrived in New York as a teenager with the same hope of becoming a nurse. During the depression Mom struggled just to survive and sent whatever meager money she made back home to Ireland to help bring her brother and sister over to join her. In the years to come she went on to live a long and triumphant life in New York City. She never did finish those courses to become a nurse. Maybe Leocadia Rodriguez will.

> **What though the radiance**
> **which was once so bright**
> **Be now for ever taken from my sight,**
> **Though nothing can bring back the hour**
> **Of splendour in the grass,**
> **of glory in the flower;**
> **We will grieve not, rather find**
> **Strength in what remains behind.**

William Wordsworth

Not long after my brother, my sister and I left
the old neighborhood, Mom and Pop left too. They
moved to an apartment right on the boardwalk
at Beach 123rd Street in Belle Harbor facing the
Atlantic Ocean. Pop retired in 1968 at 62. Mom
became an active member of St. Francis de
Sales parish as she had been at Sacred Heart parish
in the Bronx. She flourished as a community leader
and was elected Irish Woman of the Year and
Grand Marshall of the Rockaway St. Patrick's Day
parade in 1988.

On the day my mother was feted as Irishwoman of the year in Rockaway Beach. On her right is her sister, my Aunt Margaret. On her left my cousin Dolores McLoughlin Brush; her husband Charlie is reflected in the mirror.

Mom getting ready to lead the annual Rockaway Beach St. Patrick's Day Parade as the Grand Marshall in 1988 with a couple of local elected officials by her side.

I have wonderful memories of that Belle Harbor apartment. As we sat at her little dining room table which faced out to the expansive ocean and blue sky, I would often say, "Mom, I've visited homes in Malibu Beach and the views are not much different than the view you have here." And she would respond in her soft Irish accent, "Ah, well, I like sitting here quietly sometimes just watching the ocean. It changes every day, the water does, and I find it peaceful watching the waves coming in and going out under the big sky above."

On most weekends in the summers from 1972 through 1982 when my children were growing up, I took them to Mamie's house in Belle Harbor. We set up the beach blanket and umbrella and played all day long on the beach. Mom would arrive with sandwiches and sodas in the mid-afternoon. I can still see her trudging through the sand from her apartment with double bags of food and drinks as the sunlight shined down on her.

I remember a particular day. I am standing on the shore as my Sean and Jenny gambol about in the surf. A quiet joy, a calm delight, sweeps through me as the little waves lap at my ankles, and I gaze out at my two children bravely riding the glittering waves. For ones so young they appear fearless and insist on staying in the surf far longer than I ever did. After a while, I dive into the water to join them. The sun

glistens off their bodies as the three of us roll gently with the waves beyond the sounds of the shoreline. A calmness reigns — father, son, and daughter together in the sea — and my 9 year old Sean with a shining smile on his face turns to me as I hold his sister Jennifer in my arms and he says, "Dad, this is peace, isn't it?" I smile in wonderment at the wisdom of his young self.

That scene of Sean and Jennifer from long ago came back to me again though the place was different. I am a 72 year old grandfather and my two children have come to visit me and my dear Mary Anne at our country home in Columbia County, New York. Sean and Jennifer and their mates, Rebecca and Bronson, and our four grandchildren Delilah, Brian, Keira and Ravenna visit the beach at Lake Taconic State Park. I sit on a beach chair under a maple tree. Next to me in her little cradle is infant Ravenna. The others are playing in the water. I gaze on them as I once gazed on Sean and Jenny when they were little children in Belle Harbor. There's my gray-haired son, Sean, now in his mid 40's, holding his little girl, Keira, and there's Bronson teaching his daughter Delilah to swim; there's Rebecca and Jennifer watching the handsome little 4 year old Brian paddling about in the water by the shoreline, gaining the attention of a group of older girls.

My son Sean and my daughter Jennifer in the days when they first started visiting their grandmother and grandfather at Belle Harbor.

How can a man not think at times like this of the cycle of life, the ebb and flow, the comings and goings, the passing of time, the old giving way to the new, the circle unbroken? As I look upon those young parents I think of the struggles ahead of them, of the glad times and the sad times, of the hopes and dreams for themselves and their little ones. And I think too of Mom and Pop – long gone now – and their time on their beach and how young they once were and how courageous they were to leave their native land to start a new life in America. How much they gave to us and how this book I am trying to write is my attempt to keep them with us a little longer.

CPSIA information can be obtained
at www.ICGtesting.com
Printed in the USA
JSHW042312230521
15138JS00001B/2

9 780989 565615